Lineberger Memorial Library

Lutheran Theological Southern Seminary    Columbia, S. C.

# A Chick Called Saturday

# A Chick Called

For Chrissie Church, with love
J.D.

To my two little cockerels!
B.G.

# Saturday

Joyce Dunbar  *Illustrated by* Brita Granström

EERDMANS BOOKS FOR YOUNG READERS
Grand Rapids, Michigan • Cambridge, U.K

Mother Hen had seven little chicks.

They were called

Sunday,

Monday,

Tuesday,

Wednesday,

Thursday,

Friday,

and

# Saturday

in that order, because they had hatched in that order.

When the chicks were old enough Mother Hen took them for their very first walk round the farmyard.

"Follow me. Keep in line. And don't talk to any strange animals."

The seven chicks did as they were told, all except one, the chick called Saturday.

He wanted to stop and talk to all the strange animals and the strange insects and the strange objects that he saw on the farm. He wanted to talk to them all.

"Saturday!" clucked his mother.

"Get in line!" For the moment,

Saturday did as he was told.

"Now, this is the pond," said Mother Hen to her chicks. "It is full of water. Water is very wet. Nasty stuff, except for drinking. You must keep away from it."

Six little chicks shivered as they looked at the water and crept close to their mother.

But not Saturday. Oh no. Saturday edged right down to the water.

There were some strange creatures there, doing strange things.

"What are they?" Saturday asked his mother.

"Ducks," said his mother.

"What are they doing?" asked Saturday.

"Swimming," said his mother.

"What else?" asked Saturday.

"Bobbing. Swimming
and bobbing."

"When can *I* do that?"
asked Saturday.

"Never," said his mother.

"Never?" asked Saturday.

"Not ever!" said his mother.

"Now, get in line."

The seven little chicks followed their mother to a field.

Strange creatures came to greet them, hissing and honking loudly.

Six little chicks backed away, but not Saturday.

He stared at them, beak to beak.

"What are they?" Saturday asked his mother.

"Geese."

"What are they doing?" asked Saturday.

"Hissing and honking," said his mother.

"What else?" asked Saturday.

"Showing off," said his mother.

"When can *I* do that?" asked Saturday.

"Never," said his mother.

"Not ever! Now, keep in line."

Just then, Saturday saw another strange creature flutter to a fence post. He watched as it flew to the tree tops. He listened as it sang a merry song.

"What's that?"
he asked his mother.
"A blackbird,"
said his mother.
"What is it doing?"
asked Saturday.
"Flying," said his mother.
"Flying and singing a song."
"When can *I* do that?"
asked Saturday.
"Never," said his mother. "Not ever!"

"Well, what *can* I do?" asked Saturday.

"Oh lots of things," said his mother.

"What things?" asked Saturday.

"You can keep in line for a start,"
said his mother.

"What else?" asked Saturday.

"You can cluck! You can scratch!
You can peck!" said his mother.

"You can pull a worm if you try!"

"What else?" asked Saturday.

"You can stop asking questions," said his mother.

"Is that all?" asked a very sad Saturday.

Saturday was very disappointed. Clucking was all very well.
Scratching was all very well. Pecking was all very well. He might
even try to pull a worm. But there had to be more to life.

"There is more! I know it!" said Saturday. And he made up
his mind to find out for himself.

$O$n Monday he sneaked away to the pond. He launched himself onto the water and tried to swim and bob with all the little ducklings.

But he didn't have the right kind of feet. He didn't have the right kind of feathers. His feet couldn't paddle and his feathers got wet.

"Chook!" he said miserably, dragging himself out of the water while all the ducks *quack quacked*.

"Just look at you!" clucked his mother.

"The state of you!"
clucked his mother.

On Tuesday he sneaked off to the field. He joined all the goslings and tried his best to honk and hiss.

But he could only go "chook chook" and the goslings trampled him into the mud.

On Wednesday, Saturday managed to scramble onto the back of the pig while she was snoozing in her sty.

"This is high," said Saturday.

On Thursday, Saturday managed to hop onto the sheep's back where she was grazing in the field. "This is higher," said Saturday.

On Friday, Saturday managed to climb onto the cow's back where she was staring and flicking her tail. "This is so high," said Saturday. "High enough to fly!"

He tried to do just that while singing a merry song.

Plop!

Straight into a cowpat.

"The smell of you!" clucked his mother.

On Saturday, Saturday was glum. He was following his mother in line with the others when…

perched on a wall…

he saw…

the most amazing creature of all!

It had a dangly red beard. It had a curved golden beak. It had a great flounce of tail feathers, in midnight blue, bronze, and scarlet. It was flecked with sea-foam white. It had jewel-like eyes and a magnificent red crown on its head.

Saturday eyed the creature. The creature eyed him.

# Suddenly…

Cock-a-doodle-doo!

went the creature.

Saturday puffed out his feathers. He stretched

out his neck. He stood as tall as he could.

went Saturday.

"Well I never!" clucked his very proud mother.

"The sound of you!"

This edition published in 2003 by Eerdmans Books for Young Readers
an imprint of Wm B. Eerdmans Publishing Co.
255 Jefferson Ave. S.E.,
Grand Rapids, Michigan 49503
P.O. Box 163, Cambridge CB3 9PU U.K.

Created, designed, and produced by by Doubleday,
an imprint of Random House Children's Books

Text copyright © Joyce Dunbar 2003
Illustrations copyright © Brita Granström 2003

Designed by Ian Butterworth

1 2 3 4 5 6 7 8 9 08 07 06 05 04 03

ISBN 0-8028-5260-2

A catalog record of this book is available from the Library of Congress.

Printed and bound in Singapore by Tien Wah Press